Pilates

Wall Pilates for Seniors to Enhance
Flexibility and Balance

*(An Illustrated Guide to Improve Your Posture
and Build Your Core Strength)*

Todd Barcomb

Published By **Elena Holly**

Todd Barcomb

Pilates: Wall Pilates for Seniors to Enhance Flexibility and Balance (An Illustrated Guide to Improve Your Posture and Build Your Core Strength)

ISBN   978-1-9992123-6-0

No part of this guidebook shall be reproduced in any form without permission in writing from the publisher except in the case of brief quotations embodied in critical articles or reviews.

Legal & Disclaimer

The information contained in this book is not designed to replace or take the place of any form of medicine or professional medical advice. The information in this book has been provided for educational & entertainment purposes only.

The information contained in this book has been compiled from sources deemed reliable, and it is accurate to the best of the Author's knowledge; however, the Author cannot guarantee its accuracy and validity and cannot be held liable for any errors or omissions. Changes are periodically made to this book. You must consult your doctor or get professional medical advice before using any of the suggested remedies, techniques, or information in this book.

Table Of Contents

Chapter 1: What Is Classical Pilates?

Pilates is a series of managed bodily video games with the reason to construct a sturdy middle (Powerhouse), to beautify posture and alignment and to beautify flexibility of the spine and limbs. Pilates is meant as a whole frame exercising and become originated via Joseph Pilates. The mixture of the managed wearing sports and the breath makes Pilates not first-rate a bodily exercising but it additionally stimulates intellectual interest, growing that link amongst body and thoughts. When we communicate of Classical Pilates we are speakme approximately the conventional manner Joseph Pilates created the bodily sports activities now not to be careworn with Pilates being practiced in a lecture room (think about the time period classical in classical tune). Although Classical Pilates does often take place in a take a look at room or studio. Classical Pilates has a fixed collection of sports activities for beginners, intermediate and superior stages. In this e-book we're actually focussing on the beginners exercises. Joseph Pilates created this set order of sporting sports due to the truth he believed those sporting sports complimented each different and counter stretched every distinct, so the schooling is probably a balanced universal exercising and may create the exquisite effects.

Joseph Pilates

Joseph Pilates end up born in 1883 in Germany. His father modified right into a gymnast and this sparked his fascination for bodily movement. Joseph became frequently ill and he decided to come to be a gymnast and bodybuilder like his father and devoted his whole lifestyles to enhance his fitness and health. During this time he developed the belief that terrible posture, terrible respiration and the stress of ordinary existence became the idea of horrific physical and intellectual fitness. With this in thoughts he advanced a sequence of sporting sports. Joseph moved to England and made a living as a boxer and self-defence instructor at numerous police schools. During World War 1 Joseph had been given interned with the useful resource of the British authorities and during this imprisonment he skilled his fellow internees. This is in which he definitely diffused his physical games walking with the limited system in his prison environment and he began out calling his workout contrology. When he grow to be launched he first went lower back to Germany in which he started out walking with professionals in physical fitness and dance. After that he moved to the usa. On his way to the States he met his spouse Clara and they opened their first Pilates studio in NYC. Because of the collaboration with dance experts, most of his first clients were dancers. Joseph stored finessing his sporting sports. He moreover

3

have grow to be inspired thru the motion of animals. With all this data he created the Classical Pilates sports sports that we apprehend these days and that we get to examine on this ebook. At the age of 80 3, Joseph Pilates past away in New York (in 1967).

Powerhouse

We have already said the Powerhouse in financial disaster 1. But what is going to we suggest via way of it?

The Powerhouse in Classical Pilates way:

Mainly the abdominals (4 layers)

1.Transversus abdominis (internal maximum layer)

2. Internal Obliques (element abdominals 2nd layer)

3. External Obliques (aspect abdominals third layer)

Rectus abdominis (outer layer six %)

The inner thighs

The butt muscle groups

going for walks together as a strong unit.

All bodily video video games in Classical Pilates are initiated from the Powerhouse (predominantly the abdominals) and are to bolster the Powerhouse. Joseph Pilates believed that all correct movement start from the Powerhouse and therefore he believed that having a robust Powerhouse creates sturdiness of the frame.

four. The 6 Pilates requirements

Joseph Pilates created all his sports activities with 6

standards in thoughts.

Concentration

Control

Centering

Precision

Breathing

Flow

Concentration

As you may look at on this e-book, Classical Pilates carrying activities and transitions from one exercise to the alternative, are very unique. That is why reputation is one of the pilates standards to accumulate the first-class consequences of each exercising you carry out. The concept of interest sounds so smooth but out of my personal experience I surely have moments I am doing something and I am completely thinking about a few issue else. In those moments I am not focussed on the project that I am doing and that regularly indicates within the consequences. The results are regularly now not as nicely as once I am really focussed. The same goes for working closer to Classical Pilates. The extra you workout recognition and hobby the better you get at it and the higher the results of your Pilates practice is probably. Not truly on a bodily degree but additionally on a highbrow degree.

Control

When we practice Pilates, masses of factors come collectively.

We want to don't forget:

our breath

what our limbs are doing

attractive our Powerhouse

the real motion of the exercise

coordination

taking note of corrections and rhythm

To be capable of do the sporting sports to the first-class of your ability, except concentrating we really need a remarkable manner to control our our bodies to carry a majority of these factors together. This is some thing that still comes with exercise and familiarity with the sports activities.

Centering

As we already talk all Classical Pilates sports activities are initiated from the Powerhouse, the centre of the frame. We begin the workout with centering the thoughts (interest) and the body. As we lay down at the mat earlier than we begin our bodily sports activities, we want to make certain we are centered on the mat. We art work our limbs identical distance from the centreline. We moreover start our wearing activities near the centreline and as we beautify and benefit manipulate we can flow into greater a ways from the centreline. (Example legs inside the loads, the more enhance the decrease the legs, the legs bypass some distance from the centre of the frame.)

Precision

Precision stands in step with attention and manage. We use our hobby and manipulate to execute the bodily video games with the fine precision of our functionality. In Classical Pilates we're very precise approximately the repetitions of each exercising because of the reality we attention more at the outstanding of the physical sports than the quantity. We need to make certain that the body doesn't get exhausted and begins to compensate with particular muscle groups and joints that are not the purpose of the exercise. We want to execute the exercising with the wonderful precision, enticing the Powerhouse and getting the exceptional results. Therefore precision is one of the 6 principals in Classical Pilates.

Breathing

Joseph Pilates believed that terrible respiratory turned into one of the elements for terrible health. Breathing is very critical for the blood waft and for the cells in the body to art work in an maximum reliable way. Also exhaling facilitates to certainly agreement the abdominals and growing a hyperlink amongst body and thoughts. Using the breath in Classical Pilates sporting sports furthermore creates go along with the go along with the go with the flow within the physical sports. In Pilates we mainly use pinnacle ribs and once more respiration in preference to decrease belly respiratory this way we will hold our abdominals shrunk as deep as possible growing a robust Powerhouse for each exercise to paintings from. We generally inhale in extension and exhale in flexion (contraction) and in twisting (rotation). Example: in exercise Spine stretch ahead we inhale whilst we sit straight away (extension) we exhale even as we gain earlier up and over (flexion).

Flow

As an awful lot as Pilates is set precision and manage we additionally need to create flowing movement through combining the breath with the movement. Pilates is supposed as a workout with all said above in mind. As quick as we installation the exercising and the 5 unique principle we want to encompass the waft. Moving from exercising to exercise with the suitable transition making the Pilates exercising one huge flowing workout that ideally maintains going until you reach the Push up collection on the surrender. This is what we art work within the path of. But in case you're running with novices you'll should prevent occasionally to provide an purpose behind or in case you need to zoom in to some of the wearing activities. The extra superior the more flowing the exercise is probably. I do want to say that even in case you are working with beginners you still want to find out some flow in the workout so the magnificence will however be a workout. This may be tough for the trainer at the begin however with right coaching and revel in it will get much much less hard.

Teachers talents

When I first started as a Pilates trainer I already had masses of experience coaching dance. As a dance instructor you need to expose each move so your university students are capable of select out up the choreography. In Classical Pilates all the coaching is verbal and without song. You will use your voice because the device for the whole magnificence. This is probably the maximum difficult thing whilst you begin teaching Pilates.

Basic beauty information

Usually a Classical Pilates beauty is 50-60 min. We workout Classical Pilates on each a yoga mat or on a specialized Pilates mat, which might be commonly masses thicker. We start and end our Pilates Practice in Pilates stance. Teaching our university college students correct posture on the equal time as we start the beauty. The cause is that the students will stroll out of the magnificence energised and with first-class posture. That's why we moreover stop the beauty standing in Pilates stance.

Chapter 2: Teach Out Of Your Powerhouse

As a Pilates teacher it is truly critical that you teach from you Powerhouse. This technique from the immediately your university university students stroll in the elegance and the moments you are schooling the class, till they stroll out of the beauty you may lead with the beneficial resource of instance showing extraordinary posture your self. You can't say "straighten your returned lengthy" in your college students whilst you yourself are taking walks spherical with a slouch.

Use your voice

Besides coaching out of your Powerhouse you want to also be privy to your voice. As the Classical Pilates class is specially verbally taught be aware of the quantity or the dynamics of your voice. The cause is to provide your students a workout but you furthermore may want to make it fun so they'll come decrease returned. You can growth the quantity and dynamic or rhythm of your voice whilst you need to inspire your university students in a difficult exercise. Or you can calm the voice a bit at the identical time as you begin and end the elegance. Make positive your college college students can pay attention you nicely in order that they understand what to do or what to attention on.

Giving corrections

During the class you can additionally offer your college students corrections. Give at the least 2 or 3 verbal corrections for each workout!! This is to stimulate your college students so you can do the exercise as unique as feasible. There are 3 strategies to accurate your university students.

Verbally

By contact

By demonstrating

Verbally

When you verbally accurate your college college students I would like to inspire you to correct in the affirmative. What I suggest thru that is that you verbalise what you need to look or inspire in preference to what you don't want your college students to do.

For instance: Instead of announcing "don't arch your lower decrease returned within the loads".

You could say: "pull your abs in the direction of your spine to plant the decrease back into the mat".

So you're directing your college college students to the best posture in the exercise.

By touch

When you operate contact as a way to correct you college college students, you genuinely want to understand as a instructor. Because not anyone likes to be touched. Before you contact a person to correct them you may ask them or you may gradually touch. With a gradual touch I advise beginning with a moderate touch to warn them that you will accurate them and then use a bit extra strain frequently. You actually need to be practical with the firmness of your contact. There is not some thing worse than a hint this is like a tickle or a hint this is too enterprise. So really use your common revel in whilst the use of contact. Also while you go with the flow and make contact with a person actually recognise what you are attempting to advantage with the touch. If unsure don't contact and in reality deliver them a verbal correction or an instance.

Demonstration

As we stated earlier than Classical Pilates is taught verbally. The cause for this is that the students can paintings inner their very personal potential and now not attempt to reproduction the trainer and strain them selves inside the exercising and potentially injure them selves. Pilates is a method, the extra you exercise the better you could get. That being said there are moments within the class that you could reveal one or bodily sports to expose the precision or caution of an workout. But we goal to try this as low as viable.

Smart use of phrases

As we've got had been given stated earlier than, Classical Pilates is specially verbally taught. Because Classical Pilates is meant to be a workout we would like to maintain the go together with the waft within the class. A way to gain that is to be simply clever with the words you use. Try to be as brief and unique possible together collectively together with your words. For instance: Instead of saying "And now we are going to bend our knees in the chest to installation for the Hundreds". You need to say "Bend knees in chest for the Hundreds". Try to locate quick cuts to get your college college students in that you need them, so you have extra time to correct them and attention on go together with the flow and precision. This is some element with a purpose to be hard at the start. But I would love to indicate you to do an ordeal elegance with friends or circle of relatives to exercise this very vital capacity. This will in truth make the difference in turning into a amazing Classical Pilates teacher.

Fun teacher

The shape and physical sports activities of Classical Pilates are very precise, this may doubtlessly make the beauty very rigid. Even tho you need to paste to the order and format you moreover mght need to make the class amusing and smooth going so humans will come lower lower returned. Work difficult and make your students art work difficult but additionally play a touch bit. Make jokes or use imaginitive terms to inspire your students to get into the right posture. For instance: Instead of announcing "Squeeze your butt muscle companies". You may also want to mention "maintain directly to a $a hundred with butt". Your university students will even though have interaction their butt muscular tissues however it offers the workout some lightness and amusing.

Also bear in thoughts that we all have horrible days from time to time but on the same time as you are schooling a class I would love to inspire you to hold in mind that you are there to be in carrier of your college students. You are there to encourage them and to teach them some component fantastic. Try to move away your terrible day trip of the school room. Your college students will every now and then have a awful day as well. Really be sensible of the energy of the business enterprise and adjust as a consequence. Have a touch conversation along side your college students after the beauty and usually be uplifting and motivating.

6. Pilates stance, teachers posture and warmth up bodily sports activities

Pilates stance

When we begin our exercise we want to ensure that we installation an aligned feature from which we're capable of paintings from. In Classical Pilates we call that position Pilates stance.

Let's analyse the Pilates stance from backside to top.

Feet are in a V function, the toes are 2 fist width apart,

heels touch.

The legs are straight away, the knees aren't over stretched or

bend, knees are pulled up towards the thighs

The thighs contact and are became around to the element

The butt muscle mass are squeezed collectively

The abs are pulled in within the path of the backbone

The again is right now

The ribs are pulled in

The palms are beside the body and the shoulders are

down pulled in to the shoulder blades

Both shoulders are at the same degree

Chest is massive and open

Neck is prolonged

Chin is parallel to the ground, you may healthful a fist amongst

chest and chin

Gaze is earlier

Top of the top reaches in the direction of the ceiling

This is the correct evaluation of the Pilates stance. But you will revel in that your college university students may moreover have first-rate postures. You may additionally have a student to your beauty that has knocked knees. This individual received't be capable of maintain the heels collectively while standing in Pilates stance. In this situation you ensure that the scholars works inside their functionality. As a instructor you have got on the manner to realize those postures and preserve in thoughts that you are not pushing your scholar right proper right into a posture they anatomically can't do. This is why it's very important to have a take a look at and memorise certain postures and to do a little self have a look at of the human anatomy.

Teachers posture

It is critical as a instructor to teach from your Powerhouse and apprehend of your posture at the same time as you are training. The

Pilates stance paperwork the bottom to your instructors posture. You is probably walking across the studio at the same time as you teach. Are you walking around collectively collectively together with your abs pulled in? Are you status alongside facet your knees overstretched? You can in truth take a look at your very personal posture via the usage of the pointers of the proper Pilates stance on the previous pages. I am not announcing which you want to stroll round collectively together with your toes in a V function all of the time but it certainly lets in to study your very very own posture and discover wherein and the way you could beautify your instructors posture. This way you may moreover be a amazing example and thought on your university university college students.

Warm up physical video games

Before beginning with the whole Classical Pilates beginners order, you could pick out to do 2 or three warm temperature up sports activities. And if you have enough time you could select out to do 1 or 2 sports on the prevent of the elegance. These heat up bodily video games are little snippets from some of the general Classical Pilates bodily sports. This way your university college students already are acquainted with fine postures. So the goal for those heat up sports activities sports are not just to warm up the frame however are also to exercise and enhance some of the vital trouble factors of the whole Classical Pilates order. For instance a way to engage the abs or a way to keep the ribs in when lifting the hands subsequent to the ears. We will communicate a few pointers of sports that you could use. It is perfectly fine to add your very personal warm up sporting activities however simply ensure that they may be no longer sincerely there to warmth up your scholar, but that you use carrying sports with a deeper reason, so that it will praise and improve the bodily activities inside the complete Classical Pilates order.

Standing warmness up sports activities

Some of these carrying events you can use earlier than you start the masses or on the quit of the class. I will point out with each exercise, in which within the exercising I would possibly recommendation you to do the exercise. For greater statistics to help your Classical Pilates adventure discover a majority of those heat up wearing sports within the motion images at the Classical PIlates Youtube Channel.

Head rolls

Start in Pilates stance and roll the top to the proper 4 or

five instances and then repeat to the left

Head moves in isolation of the rest of the frame

Keep the abs pulled within the route of the spine

Do this exercising earlier than you begin the full workout

Goals: Warming up the neck

Shoulder rolls

Start in Pilates stance and roll the shoulder decrease back 4 or 5

instances after which repeat to the front

Shoulders float in isolation of the rest of the frame

Keep the abs pulled in the direction of the spine

Do this workout earlier than you begin the overall workout

Goals: Warming up the shoulders, warming up the better decrease decrease again

Arm isolations

Start in Pilates stance lifting the hands closer to the ceiling subsequent to the ears after which accumulate to the aspect.

Chapter 3: Bending The Knees Barely

Rounding the backbone backwards, take a look at belly button

Then arching the backbone returned, look as a good buy due to the fact the ceiling

Repeat 4 to five times

Keep the abs engaged

Shoulders down

Use your breath

Do this exercise before you start the whole exercise or at

the stop of the elegance

Goals: Warming up the lower returned and ribs, will boom flexibility of the backbone

Hip isolations

Start with the legs barely wider than the hips, legs

parallel

Bending the knees slightly

Lifting the pelvis ahead and lower back and side to facet

Repeat 4 to eight times

Move the hips in isolation from the relaxation of the frame

Keeping the abs engaged

Do this exercising earlier than you start the whole exercising or at

the stop of the class

Goals: Warming up the decrease over again, warming up the hips, will boom flexibility within the decrease decrease lower back and hips

Hip circles

Start with the legs slightly wider than the hips, legs

parallel

Bending the knees barely

Circling the hips 4 to five times and then circle the hips in

opposite path

Move the hips in isolation from the relaxation of the frame

Keeping the abs engaged

Do this exercising earlier than you start the whole exercising or at

the prevent of the magnificence

Goals: Warming up the lower lower back, warming up the hips, increase flexibility within the decrease lower again and hips

Roll down

Start in Pilates stance

Reaching arms in the course of the ceiling

Articulate spine all of the way down and once more up

Repeat three to 4 instances

When hamstring are tight bend the legs at the same time as rolled

down

Keep the abs engage

Keep the pelvis however as long as feasible when rolling

down

Do this exercising earlier than you begin the whole exercise or at

the give up of the elegance

Goals: Warming up the returned, spine flexibility, learn how to

articulate the spine, hamstring stretch

Squats parallel and turned out

Start with the legs barely wider than the hips, legs

parallel or barely wider and grew to come to be out

Then bend the legs at the equal time as maintaining the lower lower returned as at once

as feasible

Repeat 4 to 6 instances

When bending the legs the thighs are parallel

to the ground

Keeping the abs engaged

Squeeze the butt muscle corporations at the same time as straightening the legs

Do this exercise earlier than you begin the whole exercise or at

the cease of the magnificence

Goals: Warming up the legs, strengthening legs and

butt muscle groups

Ballet plié (Ballet squats)

Start the exercising in a Ballet first role (take a look at

terminology listing)

Hands within the waist

Bending the legs 1/2 of manner retaining the lower returned immediately

(heels on the floor) and then bend all of the manner down

lifting the heels barely and are available all over again up

Repeat four to six instances

When you bend the legs 1/2 of of way preserve heels at the

ground

The lower you go relies upon on how right away you may

preserve your lower back, the cause is to preserve the again as immediately

as viable

Do this exercising in advance than you start the complete exercising or at

the prevent of the splendor

Goals: Warming up the legs, strengthening legs and

butt muscle corporations

Forced arch

Start in a parallel function each hip width or collectively

or somewhere in among

Or begin in Pilates stance

Lift the heels and come at the ball of the foot one via manner of

one or each at the equal time

Repeat 4 to 8 times

Keeping the higher body as despite the reality that as possible

Keeping the abs engaged

Keeping the butt muscle tissues engaged

Do this workout before you begin the overall exercise or at

the end of the splendor

Goals: Warming up the feet, strengthening legs, butt muscle tissue and calfs, balance exercising

Balance bodily sports

Start parallel feet together or in Pilates stance

Lift one leg up preserving the alternative foot flat on the

ground or come to the ball of the foot for added superior

Hold the stability for 10 counts

When you preserve for 10 counts you can look to the proper

then left then up after which down

Do this exercise earlier than you start the whole exercising or at the stop of the elegance

Goals: Strengthening the abs, will growth popularity and

manipulate

Seated and supine warmness up carrying sports

Most of these bodily video video games I use before the hundreds. But there are some exceptions. Let's have a have a examine the ones physical video games.

Baby roll once more

Start in a seated role with the knees bend and ft

parallel flat on the mat

Hold without delay to the thighs

And roll again straightening the hands aiming to the touch

the decrease all over again on the mat and roll lower again up

Keeping the abs pulled in

Repeat four times

Keep the backbone in a C curve even as you roll lower lower lower back up,

straighten the lower back only at the very last second

Keep looking within the stomach

Do this exercising in advance than you begin the total exercise

Goals: Activating the lower abs, strengthening the decrease abs, warming up the frame, operating in the direction of preserving the lower lower back in a C curve

Baby roll again to flat once more

Start in a seated characteristic with the knees bend and toes

parallel flat at the mat

Hold right away to the thighs back is straight away appearance forward

And roll once more look in the belly straightening the hands

aiming to the touch the lower returned at the mat and roll

lower lower again as a good buy as a right away once more and look up

Keeping the abs pulled in

Repeat 4 times

Keep the backbone in a C curve at the same time as you roll lower once more up

Keep looking within the stomach

Do this exercise before you start the entire workout

Goals: Activating the decrease abs, strengthening the lower abs, warming up the body, operating in the path of the difference

among immediately again and a C curve

Arm isolations

Start in a supine function with the knees bend and ft

parallel flat at the mat

Reaching fingers to the ceiling, then reaching the fingers

next to the ears

Repeat four to six times

Keep the ribs pulled in

Keep the abs engaged

Keep the lower again inside the mat

Shoulder are pulled inside the all over again

Do this exercise earlier than you begin the overall exercise

Goals: Warming up shoulders, studying a way to pass the fingers in isolation from the relaxation of the body, gaining knowledge of to achieve the arms subsequent to the ears without flaring up the ribs

Arm isolations in desk top

Start in a supine position with the knees bend on a 90º

mindset, legs together, issue the toes parallel

Reaching fingers to the ceiling, then accomplishing the arms

next to the ears

Repeat four to six instances

Keep the ribs pulled in

Keep the abs engaged

Keep the lower once more within the mat

Shoulder are pulled inside the lower once more

Do this exercising in advance than you start the general exercising

Goals: Warming up shoulders, reading the manner to move the fingers in isolation from the rest of the body, reading to attain the hands subsequent to the ears without flaring up the ribs, activating the decrease abs, getting to know to hold the decrease all over again inside the mat

Dead bug

Start in a supine feature with the knees bend on a 90º

mindset, legs collectively, point the toes parallel

Reaching hands to the ceiling

Then reap proper arm next to the ear and straighten

left leg on the identical time, come lower lower back, then repeat

opposite arm and leg

Repeat 4 to 6 instances

Keep the ribs pulled in

Keep the abs engaged

Keep the lower again within the mat

Shoulder are pulled inside the lower again

Do this workout before you begin the whole exercising

Goals: Warming up shoulders, studying the way to flow into the palms in isolation from the rest of the body, analyzing to attain the hands subsequent to the ears with out flaring up the ribs, activating the decrease abs, reading to hold the lower once more in the mat, improve coordination

Hip isolations

Start in a supine function with the knees bend and feet

parallel flat at the mat

Legs are hip width apart

Lifting the hips to the ceiling, then arching the returned

Repeat 4 to six instances

Keeping the abs engaged

Moving the hips in isolation to the relaxation of the body

Do this workout before you begin the general exercise or

earlier than shoulder bridge

Goals: Warming up the lower again, boom flexibility in the decrease once more and pelvis

Alternating desk top faucet

Start in a supine function with the knees bend on a 90º

mind-set, legs together, element the feet parallel

Arms are flat inside the mat achieving away inside the direction of the

feet

Tap the proper toe at the mat and lift again up repeat

with left leg

Repeat four to 6 instances

Keeping the lower again in the mat

Keeping the abs engaged

Keeping the ribs in

Do this workout earlier than you start the overall exercising

Goals: Warming up the lower abs, strengthening the lower abs, studying to keep the ribs and abs in and

maintaining the decrease once more inside the mat

Double desk pinnacle faucet

Start in a supine characteristic with the knees bend on a 90º

attitude, legs collectively, factor the ft parallel

Arms are flat within the mat reaching away closer to the

feet

Tap every toes on the mat

Repeat 4 to six instances

Keeping the decrease decrease again within the mat

Keeping the abs engaged

Keeping the ribs in

Do this exercising earlier than you begin the general exercise

Goals: Warming up the lower abs, strengthening the decrease abs, mastering to keep the ribs and abs in and retaining the lower again inside the mat

Head and shoulder enhance

Start in a supine position with the knees bend and ft

parallel flat on the mat

Arms achieving within the direction of the ceiling

Lifting head and shoulders out of the mat in among

the arms and decrease head and shoulders back off in

the mat

Variation 1: Lift head and shoulder then attain hands

subsequent to the ear decrease returned to the ceiling then lower head and

shoulder lower lower back on the mat

Variation 2: Reaching arms next to the ears raise head

and shoulder out the mat keeping the hands subsequent to the

ears and decrease head and shoulders lower returned inside the mat

Repeat 4 to 8 times

Look inside the belly at the same time as lifting up head and shoulders

Keep pulling the abs in

Keep decrease again within the mat

Do this exercise in advance than you start the whole exercise

Goals: Strengthening higher abs, warming up the abs and body

Cat and cow

Come on all fours

Rounding the backbone towards the ceiling searching in the

belly

Then arching the decrease again searching at the ceiling

Repeat 4 to eight times

Keep the abs engaged

Do this exercise after or earlier than the rest function or earlier than the frenzy up series

Chapter 4: The Full Order Of The Classical Pilates Mat Novices Carrying Activities

In this bankruptcy we will check all of the Classical Pilates Mat novices carrying sports activities. On the subsequent internet page you may discover a chart with all the wearing sports, the recommended repetitions and some extra notes. Further in this economic ruin we are able to look in to each exercise in entire intensity. All the wearing sports activities are in addition described inside the films you may find on the YouTube Channel Classical Pilates. On this YouTube Channel you may additionally find out a video with the complete order of all of the beginners sporting events.

Hundreds

Repetitions: one hundred

Inhale five pumps and exhale 5 pumps repeat 10 times (100)

Goals:

Stimulates blood movement

Warm-up of the body

Strengthens the abdominals

Lengthens the body

Set up:

Knees inside the chest

Lift head and shoulder of the mat

Lift the palms

Look in to belly button

Lengthen the legs forty five stages of the floor

Beginner obtain legs directly to the ceiling (proximal)

The lower the legs the greater supply a boost to (distal)

Ideally the legs are on eye degree (Really superior)

Feet in pilates aspect (toes in V position heels collectively

ft aside issue the toes)

Set exercise in motion:

Start pumping the palms

Breathe in 2,3,4,five

Breathe out 2,3,4,5

Corrections:

Look into stomach button

Keep lifting shoulders of the mat

Keep decrease once more glued inside the mat

Keep heels collectively

Squeeze the butt (at the equal time as legs are stretched out forty five

stages)

Keep pulling abs within the direction of the spine

Reminding the breath inhale five pumps exhale 5 pumps

Keep the pinnacle, top frame and legs nevertheless at the identical time as

pumping the palms

Notes:

The lower the legs can flow into virtually is predicated upon on if you may preserve the decrease decrease returned planted inside the mat via the usage of pulling your abs in and glueing your abs on the spine. With beginners you actually need to attain the legs extra towards the ceiling, running proximal. The extra improve they get the decrease the legs circulate, running distal. Ideally the legs should skip eye degree. Always supply knees within the chest first in advance than lifting head out of the mat in particular with beginners.

Transition in to Roll up:

Knees to the chest

Lower the pinnacle and shoulders once more within the mat

Lower the fingers over again inside the mat

Roll up

Repetitions:

5 times

Goals:

Articulation of the backbone

Increase flexibility of the backbone

Lengthening and stretching the backbone

Warm-up of the yet again and backbone

Strengthening the abdominals

Set up:

Straighten legs long at the mat

Feet flexed and parallel

Legs collectively (Legs may be hip with apart for

beginners but ideally legs collectively)

Arms achieving closer to the ceiling

Set workout in movement:

Breathe in chin closer to the chest, roll up trough the

fingers

Keep backbone in C curve reach ahead breathe out

Pull abs deeper in

Breathe in, articulate the spine lower back inside the mat

Reaching the hands subsequent to ears breathe out

Corrections:

Keep pushing heels away and push heels within the mat (at the same time as rolling up)

Shoulder stay down within the back

Keep abs pulled in in the direction of the backbone

Keep once more in C curve whilst rolling up and at the same time as rolling down

Keep lifting the ribs out of the hips whilst accomplishing up and over

Think like you are rolling up and over a big ball

This isn't a hamstring stretch but a spine stretch

When reaching the hands decrease decrease back next to the ear preserve ribs

down

Transition in to One leg circle:

Arms next to the frame within the mat

One leg circle

Repetitions:

five instances every path

Goals:

Strengthen the legs

Lubricate the hip joint

Promotes flexibility in the hips

Set up:

Right knee in chest

Keep left leg in the mat parallel, foot flexed

Straighten proper leg to ceiling

Leg is have end up out, foot is pointed

Set the exercise in movement:

Breathe in, circle proper leg towards left leg

Breathe out circle decrease returned as lots as a at once leg

After five repetitions opposite the circle

and alternate leg

Corrections:

Keep the leg at the mat engaged and foot flexed

Keep the jogging leg grew to end up out, right away and foot

pointed while circling the legs

Keep the abs and ribs pulled in

Imagine drawing a circle on the ceiling collectively along with your feet

Focus closer to the ceiling

Keep better body and hips as though as feasible

Push your triceps within the mat to help you stabilise

Transition in Rolling like a ball:

Beginners

Lift each knees into the chest

Hold without delay to the thighs and rock your self as much as a seated

position

Advanced beginners

Straighten each legs on the mat flex the toes

Arms achieving towards the ceiling

And roll as plenty as a seated feature (Like the Roll up

exercise)

Rolling like a ball

Repetitions:

8 instances

Goals:

Massaging de spine

Massaging the stress element alongside the backbone

Strengthening the abs

Promotes manage over the frame

Set up:

Hands subsequent to the buttocks and lift your self up a piece

forwards at the mat

Hold directly to the outside of the ankles

Lifting ft out of the mat toes in Pilates component (heels

together ft apart)

Knees in the direction of the shoulders (Knees are aside however

heels are together)

Making a C curve of the backbone

Looking into the stomach button

Balancing at the buttocks like a bit ball

Set the exercise in motion:

Breathe in roll again

Breathe out to move returned returned up and balance

Keep ft from the mat, pulling abs in

Corrections:

Roll onto the shoulders. Head and neck are not

touching the mat while rolling lower back!!!!!!

Keep the ball like shape at a few degree within the complete exercise

Deepen and keep the C curve of the spine

Keep the abs pulled in

Balance on the buttocks using the abs

Keep searching into the stomach button

Keep the heels collectively and the ft apart

Remind the breath

Notes:

When you've got got human beings with spinal issues collectively with scolioses you couldn't need to do that exercising. Instead you could do a roll up and down exercise with the knees bend like a managed crunch workout.

Transition in Single leg stretch:

Hold immediately to the proper ankle with the right hand

Hold directly to the proper knee with the left hand

Elbows big

Single leg stretch

5 ab series

Repetitions:

8-10 instances each aspect

Goals:

Strengthening the abs

Enhances coordination

Strengthening legs

Lengthening legs

Increses stamina

Set up:

Straighten left leg out forty five degrees (from the ground) ft

in Pilates element

Keep shielding directly to the proper decrease leg (or located hands on

the mat for guide)

Roll down keeping head and shoulder blades out of the

mat

Look in the stomach button

Set the exercising in motion:

Breathe in trade legs

Breathe out alternate legs and trade and change and so on.

Corrections:

Keep the head and shoulders out of the mat

The lower the proper away leg the more beautify

Keep keeping at once to the bend leg retaining the leg in to

the chest

Pull the abs in maintain them glued to the spine

Keep your lower decrease again planted within the mat!!!

Keep looking in to the belly button

Foot of heterosexual leg is in Pilates pointe (have become out)

other foot is parallel point

Reaching the proper away leg away

Elbows stay huge shoulders down

Keep the legs close to the centreline of the body and

hold reminding the breath

Notes:

The position of the palms are as observe;

When you maintain on to the proper decrease leg, your right hand is on the ankle of the proper leg and the left hand is on the knee of the proper leg, elbows stay extensive to the aspect

When you change legs, your left hand is at the ankle of the left leg and the proper hand is on the left knee, elbows live sizable to the thing.

This is in that you train a chunk of arm leg coordination. With novices you could virtually preserve straight away to the knee with each hands and the extra advanced your beginners get you can embody the perfect hand positions.

The lower the legs can cross surely is based upon on if you could hold the lower returned planted in the mat thru the usage of pulling your abs in and glueing your abs on the spine. With novices you really need to gain the legs extra closer to the ceiling, running proximal. The greater enhance they get the lower the legs pass, running distal. Ideally the legs need to bypass eye level.

Transition in to Double leg stretch:

Both knees within the chest hold without delay to the ankles

Double leg stretch

five ab collection

Repetitions:

8-10 instances

Goals:

Strengthening the abs

Strengthening legs

Lengthening legs

Increases stamina

Set up:

Knees inside the chest maintain immediately to the ankles

Set the workout in motion:

Breathe in straighten arms and legs in contrary

direction at the same time

Circle the arms

Breathe out knees to chest

Hold without delay to ankles

Corrections:

Keep searching in to the belly button

Keep lower once more planted inside the mat!!!!!

Pull the abs in keep them glued to the backbone

The decrease the legs the more decorate

Keep head and shoulder out of the mat

Straighten the hands next to the ear

Really gain legs and arms away such as you need to touch

opposite partitions

Squeeze the buttocks even as you enlarge the legs away

Keep reminding the breath

Notes:

The lower the legs can bypass certainly relies upon on if you can keep the decrease once more planted in the mat thru using pulling your abs in and glueing your abs at the backbone. With beginners you actually need to advantage the legs more in the direction of the ceiling, going for walks proximal. The greater broaden they get the lower the legs go, strolling distal. Ideally the legs have to bypass eye stage.

Transition in to Scissors:

Both knees in the chest

Scissors

five ab series

Repetitions:

8-10 instances every leg

Goals:

Strengthening the abs

Strengthening legs

Lengthening legs

Stretching the legs

Increase flexibility

Stamina

Set up:

Simultaneously straighten left leg away 45 tiers

and straighten proper leg toward the nostril

Hold without delay to the right ankle

Set this exercising in motion:

Breath in barely pull proper leg to nose two times, pull pull

Breathe out exchange legs pull pull

Change pull pull, exchange pull pull

Corrections:

Keep searching in to the belly button

Keep the lower again planted inside the mat

Keep pulling the abs in and maintain them glued to the

spine

Keep the elbows large to the side

Leg are grew to grow to be out and feet in Pilates issue

Keep the legs close to the centreline of the body

Notes:

The decrease the legs can skip actually relies upon on if you can maintain the decrease lower back planted in the mat by way of pulling your abs in and glueing your abs at the backbone. With novices you really want to acquire the legs greater in the path of the ceiling, going for walks proximal. The greater improve they get the decrease the legs bypass, operating distal. Ideally the legs need to transport eye level.

Chapter 5: Both Legs Within The Course Of The Ceiling

Legs became out ft in Pilates factor

Criss go

five ab series

Repetitions:

eight-10 times each side

Goals:

Strengthening the abs specially the obliques

Strengthening legs

Lengthening legs

Strengthening the butt muscle companies

Increases stamina

Set up:

Right knee in to the chest parallel

Lower left leg forty five degrees (from the mat) leg is turned out, foot in Pilates factor

Twist your body within the course of the bend knee

Elbows large to the issue

Set the exercising in motion:

Breathe in and alternate aspect

Breathe out exchange factor

Corrections:

Keep decrease again planted within the mat

Keep the abs pulled in and stuck to the backbone

Keep lifting every shoulder blades out of the mat

Keep the legs close to the centreline of the frame

Keep the elbows giant to the element

Really make bigger the right away leg away

Keep every hips at the mat

Twist the body from the waist

Notes:

The decrease the legs can pass simply is based upon on if you may keep the decrease lower back planted in the mat via pulling your abs in and glueing your abs at the spine. With beginners you really need to reach the legs more in the direction of the ceiling, operating proximal. The greater improve they get the decrease the legs circulate, jogging distal. Ideally the legs need to head eye stage.

Transition in to Spine stretch ahead:

Both knees within the chest

Lower the head lower lower back inside the mat

More superior

Both knees within the chest

Lower the pinnacle all over again inside the mat

Straighten the legs prolonged at the mat flex feet parallel

fingers to the ceiling

Spine stretch ahead

Repetitions:

five instances

Goals:

Enhance flexibility of the spine

Stretch the backbone

Set up:

Either rock as masses as a seated function retaining right away to the

thighs

Or do a proper roll up just like the roll up exercise to a

seated characteristic

Back is immediately

Legs as massive as mat

Legs are parallel feet are flexed

Arms accomplishing ahead, shoulder top and shoulder

width

Set the workout in motion:

Breathe in make bigger taller

Breathe out gain up and over ahead

Articulating spine decrease lower back as a whole lot as a straight away lower returned breath in

Corrections:

Keep the ribs and abs pulled in

Keep the shoulders down

Keep lifting the ribs out of the hips when you attain up

and over

Keep the arms shoulder pinnacle and width while

carrying out up and over

Keep the ft flexed and the legs active

This is a stretch for the backbone now not for the hamstrings

Keep reminding of the breath

Note:

Imagine like your attaining up and over a huge ball.

Transition in to Open leg rocker prep:

When accomplishing up and over keep at once to the ankles

Pull the ft in the course of you, on the same time as you roll up, knees cross

out to the thing, palms are at the inner of the legs

Back is right now

Feet are in Pilates element

Open leg rocker prep

Repetitions:

10 seconds

or 10 counts

Goals:

Strengthens the abs

Improves stability

Improves cognizance

Improves manipulate

Set up:

Make a little C curve in lumbar spine (decrease lower again)

Open up chest

Set the exercising in motion:

First balance ft out mat

Straighten each leg (each at the same time or one at the

time)

Keep legs shoulder width and grew to turn out to be out

And balance

Corrections:

Keep C curve in lumbar spine

Legs live inside the the the front of the shoulders

Lift the chest

Gaze on the horizon

Feet are in Pilates issue

Straighten the palms

Shoulder down

Notes:

If your pupil can't straighten their legs preserve them bend. Put extra emphasise inside the pinnacle frame, the C curve inside the lumbar backbone, the gaze and the stability.

Transition in to Corkscrew:

Close the legs

Let pass of the ankles accomplishing the palms parallel alongside

the legs

Corkscrew

Repetitions:

4 instances each course

Goals:

Strengthening the abs specifically the obliques

Strengthening the legs

Strengthening the butt muscle corporations

Improves manage

Set up:

Make a C curve in the backbone

Look in stomach button

Articulate spine down within the mat

Arms planted beside body in the mat hands down

Legs attaining directly to ceiling

Legs grew to come to be inside and out Pilates element

Set the workout in movement:

Breathe in circle the legs to the proper

Breathe out legs again to the centre

Breathe in circle the legs to the left (opposite route)

Breathe out legs once more to the centre

Corrections:

Keep heels collectively whilst circling legs

The butt will supply up slightly but top frame remains

planted and notwithstanding the fact that inside the mat!!!!!

Squeeze the buttocks

Keep the hips but as an entire lot as possible

Push the triceps inside the mat to stabilise the higher frame

Ribs stay down

Relax the pinnacle and neck muscle mass

Pull the abs in hold them glued to the backbone

Imagine drawing a basketball on the ceiling (while

greater advanced and controlled believe skippy ball)

Keep recognition at the ceiling

Remind the breath

Notes:

The more advanced the larger the circle. Start with imagining drawing an orange on the ceiling, then a basketball after which a skippy ball. The greater manage the bigger the circle.

Transition in to Saw:

Rock up with without delay legs to a seated characteristic

Legs wider than the mat

Saw

Repetitions:

five instances each facet

Goals:

Stretching the backbone

Improves flexibility inside the spine

Lengthens the backbone

Set up:

Sit with legs wider than mat

Back is without delay

Both fingers achieve to the aspect hands down

Legs parallel ft are flexed

Set the exercise in motion:

Breathe in carry the ribs out hips, shoulders down

Twist to the right from the waist

Breathe out gain up and over within the course of the pinky toe

2,three

Articulate spine another time up

Then twist once more to the centre breathe in

Repeat on the alternative component

Corrections:

Keep each hips within the mat and levelled specifically at the same time as

you rotate to the element

Keep lifting up and over at the same time as you bought in advance,

don't forget carrying out up and over a large skippy ball

Keep pulling the abs in

When sitting instantly hold the ribs in and shoulders

down

Keep flexing the feet

Keep the legs strong and energetic

Keep the shoulder down

Remind the breath

Notes:

This exercise in no longer a hamstring stretch it's miles a backbone rotation and spine lengthening workout. Keep accomplishing op and over.

Transition in to Swan neck roll:

Closing the legs

Arms reaching earlier shoulder height and width

Look in to belly button curving the backbone

Initiate from the abs to roll down at the mat

Swan neck roll

Repetitions:

3 times

Lift up 2 instances without neck roll

1/three time neck roll beginning proper and opposite

Repeat this series 1-three times

Chapter 6: Backpedal

Keep the hips nonetheless on one degree, consider balancing 2 tea

cups on each component of the hip

Remind the breath

Notes:

Open up the legs hip width apart if your student has a excellent decrease lower back or decrease once more problems.

Transition in to Side kicks front & lower back:

Straighten right arm and leg

Push your self for your right element using your left bend

leg

Side kicks front & again

Side kick series

Repetitions:

five -10 instances

Goals:

Strengthening the legs and butt muscle groups

Lengthening the legs

Strengthening the abs

Promotes interest and manipulate

Set up:

Lie to your aspect aligning your self to the over again of the

mat

Straight lower back

Right hand is assisting the top left hand inside the front of

your chest within the mat to stabilise the posture

Put the legs barely within the the front of you at the mat

Flexing the right leg and foot at the mat

Lifting the left leg hip width grew to come to be out foot is in Pi

lates component

Set the exercise in motion:

Breathe in kick kick the front

Breathe out kick lighten up

And kick kick (the the front) and kick kick (decrease again)

Corrections:

Pull in the abs and push into the hand on the mat to

stabilise the posture

Initiate the kicks from the Powerhouse

Keep pinnacle frame and hips as despite the reality that as viable

Keep the legs hip height at the same time as kicking front and back

Keep pushing the heel (of the leg in the mat) in to the

mat and maintain lengthening the heel away

Keep the leg of the pinnacle leg have become out and toes pointed

Keep the neck lengthy and head straight in keeping with the

backbone

Keep lengthening every legs, each legs are lively

Keep lifting the waist out of the mat

Remind the breath

Notes:

2 small kicks to the back and front.

The similarly the leg goes is based upon on how levelled and however the hips are and it additionally depends at the capability of the student. This exercise isn't approximately how excessive the leg is going it is approximately how despite the fact that the top frame and hips may be whilst shifting the legs from the powerhouse. This exercise is all about manipulate.

Transition in to Side kicks up & down:

Heels collectively

Keep the pinnacle leg have become out and the lowest leg parallel

and flexed pushed inside the mat

Side kicks up& down

Side kick collection

Repetitions:

5 -10 instances

Goals:

Strengthening the legs and butt muscular tissues

Lengthening the legs

Strengthening the abs

Stretching the legs

Promotes reputation and control

Set up:

Heels together

Keep the pinnacle leg grew to become out and the lowest leg parallel

and flexed pushed in the mat

Set the exercising in motion:

Breathe in increase leg to ceiling

Breathe out and withstand leg back down

Corrections:

Initiate the leg motion from the Powerhouse

Keep the top frame nonetheless

Keep the hips still and levelled

Keep the top leg right away and became out and foot in

Pilates thing

Keep pushing the heel of the bottom leg in to the mat

Keep the neck prolonged and the pinnacle immediately

Remind the breathe

Notes:

The higher the leg goes relies upon on how levelled and no matter the reality that the hips are and it additionally depends at the power of the student. This workout isn't always approximately how immoderate the leg is going it's miles approximately how hundreds you may resist the leg even as it comes back down and the way however the better body and hips can be. This workout is all approximately manage. As a model you can flex the foot at the same time as resisting the leg down.

Transition in to Side kick circles:

Heels collectively

Keep the pinnacle leg have become out and the bottom leg parallel

and flexed pushed within the mat

Side kicks circles

Side kick collection

Repetition:

5-10 instances every direction

Goals:

Strengthening the legs and butt muscle tissue

Lengthening the legs

Strengthening the abs

Stretching the legs

Promotes consciousness and manage

Set up:

Heels together

Keep the top leg became out and the bottom leg parallel

and flexed driven within the mat

Set the workout in motion:

Breathe in circle the front, up, back

Breathe out and heels decrease returned together

and circle and circle and lots of others.

Reverse the circles

Correction:

Keep brushing the heels collectively at the same time as circling

Keep the top body and hips however

Initiate the motion from the Powerhouse

Keep the ribs and abs pulled in

Keep the leg that is circling grew to come to be out and foot

pointed

Keep pushing the heel of the lowest leg inside the mat

Imagine drawing a grapefruit at the wall

Remind the breath

Notes:

The greater advanced the larger the circle. Start with imagining drawing a grapefruit at the wall, then a basketball after which a skippy ball. The more manage the larger the circle.

Transition in to Side kicks inner thigh improve up & down:

Heels together

Keep the top leg have become out and the bottom leg parallel

and flexed driven within the mat

Side kicks inner thigh bring up& down

Side kick series

Repetitions:

five-10 instances

Goals:

Strengthening the legs and butt muscle mass

Lengthening the legs

Strengthening the abs

Stretching the legs

Promotes reputation and manage

Set up:

Lift left leg to ceiling

Put left foot within the front of the hips

Through the hole of the leg preserve without delay to the ankle

Reaching the proper leg lengthy at the mat foot pointed

and parallel

Set the exercise in motion:

Breathe in growth right leg up

Breathe out resist leg down

Corrections:

Initiate leg motion from the Powerhouse

Keep top body and hips regardless of the truth that

Lengthening neck and head is immediately

Keep lengthening the bottom leg and hold accomplishing

similarly away on the same time as you decrease the leg

Keep left foot planted within the mat

Chapter 7: 5 Instances Each Path

Goals:

Strengthening the legs and butt muscles

Lengthening the legs

Strengthening the abs

Stretching the legs

Promotes attention and manipulate

Set up:

Through the hole of the leg maintain without delay to the ankle

Reaching the right leg up (Just finished up and down

keep the leg up)

Set the exercising in movement:

Breathe in circle the front, lower, lower lower lower back

Breathe out and leg is all over again up

and circle and circle and so forth.

Reverse the circles

Corrections:

Initiate the leg motion from the Powerhouse

Keep the higher body and hips however

Lengthening the neck and head is right now

Keep lengthening the bottom leg and preserve carrying out

in addition while circling

Keep the left foot planted inside the mat

Remind the breath

Notes:

In this exercising you could make the circle as massive as viable preserving the stillness of the hips and higher frame in interest.

Transition in to Beats at the stomach:

Put each leg on pinnacle of every special

Heels collectively keep lifting every legs out of the mat

Beats at the stomach

Transition exercise to aspect kick series left

Repetitions:

20 beats

Goals:

Strengthening the inner thighs

Transitioning the element kick series from the proper facet to

the left issue

Set up:

Turn at the stomach

Keep lifting your legs out of the mat

Legs are grew to turn out to be out and feet in Pilates issue heels

collectively

Make a pillow of your hand and permit your forehead rest

to your hands

Pulling the abs a long way from the mat inside the route of the backbone

Set the exercise in motion:

Open and close to the legs

Touching heels collectively every instances

and a beat beat beat beat (tempo is surrender speedy)

Corrections:

Keep lifting the abs some distance from the mat towards the

spine

Keep lifting the legs out of the mat

Squeeze the butt muscle agencies

Keep the neck long

Keep lengthening the legs away

Keep the frame as nonetheless as viable handiest the legs are

transferring

Natural breath

Repeat all of the side kick series mendacity in your left factor

Turn directly to the left component and set up for Side kicks the the front & again

Transition in to Teaser one leg:

Put both legs on pinnacle of each extraordinary

Then placed the pinnacle leg bend in the lower back of you

Push your self to a seated function or to a function

mendacity down

Right leg is bend and the left leg is without delay, knees are together

Teaser one leg

Repetitions:

5 instances each leg

Goals:

Strengthening abs

Strengthening the legs

Promotes hobby and manage

Enhances flexibility of the backbone

Set up:

Come to seated function

Right leg is bend feet flat at the ground parallel

Left leg is straight away have come to be out and toes in Pilates difficulty

Knees stay glued collectively

Move bend leg similarly far from butt, retaining knees

collectively

Arms engaging in ahead in a diagonal, parallel to the

immediately leg

C curve within the spine with an open chest

Gaze to the horizon

Set the exercise in motion:

Breathe in look in to the stomach button

Breathe out while you roll down

Reach hands subsequent to the ears, ribs in

Breathe in appearance in stomach roll up

Reach arms away diagonal in advance, open the chest

gaze up

Corrections:

Keep the knees glued together the whole time

When undertaking hands decrease returned next to ears, maintain the ribs in

Keep the abs pulled in glued to the backbone

When rolling down hold searching in to stomach button

maintaining the C curve inside the backbone

When rolling up keep looking in to the stomach button

preserving the C curve in the spine

When engaging in the nice element look up and open the

chest

Keep conducting the proper away leg away

Remind the breath

Notes:

Really have a take a look at the video to observe the 2 considered one of a type transitions and set americafor the Teaser one leg. You need to have a chunk wreck earlier than you start Teaser I. First positioned each knees within the chest after which roll the top down. Ideally you need to hold right away in to the Teaser I after the Teaser one leg. This is a difficult workout so clearly reputation at the glide of this exercising. Practice your smart use of phrases.

Transition in to Teaser I:

Both legs straight accomplishing out on forty five levels from the

mat in Pilates point

Teaser I

Repetitions:

five instances

Goals:

Strengthening abs

Strengthening the legs

Promotes consciousness and manage

Enhances flexibility of the backbone

Set up:

Come to a seated characteristic

Both legs benefit up forty five tiers from the mat

Legs are became out and feet are in Pilates component

Reaching the arms diagonal, parallel to the legs

Make a C curve of the spine

Gaze is to the horizon open chest

Set the exercise in movement:

Breathe in appearance in to the belly button

Breathe out at the identical time as you roll lower back

Reach palms next to the ears, ribs in

Breathe in look in belly roll up

Reach fingers fingers diagonal ahead, open the chest

gaze up

Corrections:

Keep the heels glued collectively the entire time

When achieving arms lower back keep the ribs in

Keep the abs pulled in glued to the backbone

When rolling down maintain looking in to stomach button

retaining the C curve inside the spine

When rolling up keep looking in to the belly button

maintaining the C curve inside the spine

When sporting out the very fine thing look up and open the

chest

Keep reaching the legs away

Squeeze the butt muscular tissues

Remind the breath

Notes:

You can leave this exercising out if your college students don't have the energy yet. Let your university college students begin with the Teaser one leg simplest until they've got built the energy and stamina.

Transition in to Swimming prep:

When you roll down to your Teaser I, move without delay into

the transition

Right arm and leg right now at the mat

Bending the left leg foot parallel flat inside the mat

Left arm besides the frame, push your self to a inclined

characteristic

Swimming prep

Repetitions:

3 instances every side

Goals:

Lengthens spine

Strengthening once more muscle companies

Set up:

Lie inclined

Arms right away next to ears

Lengthen whole body in opposite direction

Legs collectively have come to be out ft in Pilates issue

Forehead in mat long neck

Set the exercise in movement:

Breathe in raise proper arm and left leg concurrently

Breath out enlarge arm and leg decrease lower back inside the mat

simultaneously

Repeat contrary arm and leg

Corrections:

Keep lifting the abs out of the mat

Keep squeezing the butt muscle groups

Keep the legs near the centreline at the same time as lifting the

leg up and down

Keep hip bones although in the mat

Neck stays long

Keep the legs have come to be out and ft in Pilates factor

Keep the body nonetheless no rocking side to aspect

Keep lengthening in contrary course

Transition in to Swimming:

Lower every arms and legs inside the mat

Forehead at the mat

Swimming

Repetitions:

10-12 times

Goals:

Lengthens backbone

Strengthening once more muscle mass

Enhances control over the frame

Chapter 8: Put Palms Subsequent To Chest

Elbows glued in waist

Forehead in mat prolonged neck

Set the workout in motion:

Lift your self to plank function (with the useful resource of pushing inside the

arms in 1 motion)

Long neck

And hold

Corrections:

Lift as an awful lot as plank in a single movement like a stiff board

Squeeze butt muscle tissues slightly tucking the hips in advance

Keep pushing top all over again to ceiling

Pull abs in preserve them glued to spine

Keep neck lengthy

Keep lengthening at a few degree in the entire spine

Legs and toes are parallel (or Pilates stance)

You may have the legs and ft together or hip width

apart

Notes:

If your pupil is not robust enough to elevate as much as plank in 1 motion let them located their knees down and then enhance as a whole lot as plank retaining their knees on the mat.

Transition in to Mermaid stretch:

Put the proper knee at the mat, knee handling the difficulty

of the mat

Bend the left knee and sit down down down on the proper buttocks

Both knees bent on the left factor of the body

Mermaid stretch

Repetitions:

2-three times every aspect

Goals:

Stretches the facet of the frame

Stretches the hip

Set up:

Sit totally on rights buttocks

Both legs bent, on pinnacle of each exclusive, to the left factor of

the body

Hold directly to ankles with left hand

Straighten proper arm right now to ceiling glued to ear

Shoulders down

Set the workout in movement:

Breathe in enlarge ribs out hips

Breathe out attain up and over to the left aspect of frame

Breathe in come again to right now over again, each hands to the

detail

Then attain left arm to ceiling glued to ear

Breathe out supply up and over to the right aspect of the

body, setting right arm at the mat

Breathe in to move lower back lower lower back to a right now over again hands to the

thing

Transition the mermaid to take a seat at the left buttocks:

Put fingers in the back of you

Teaser the legs to the right aspect of the body

Repeat exercising on the other facet

Corrections:

Keep lifting the ribs out of the hips, mainly on the equal time as

you reach up and over

Imagine going up and over a massive skippy ball

Keep the shoulders down at the equal time as you enhance the arm to the

ceiling

The reason is to keep every butt cheeks on the mat

Keep pushing decrease again closer to the opportunity buttocks

Remind the breath

Transition in to Seal:

Put both palms in the decrease back of you

Teaser the legs to the the the front of the mat

Seal

Repetitions:

8 times

Goals:

Strengthens the abs

Cooldown

Massage of the backbone

The clapping of the ft can open strength blocks in the body and stimulates the blood glide

Set up:

Sit with ft collectively and knees open to the facet

Hold right away to the out of doors of the feet, with the aid of the usage of going through the

hole of the legs

Make a C curve of the spine at the same time as lifting each toes out

the mat

Look in to the stomach

Abs are pulled in glued to the backbone

Set the workout in motion:

Clap the toes 2,3 (clap ft three times)

Breathe in roll again and clap 2,three

Breathe out to roll up and balance

Corrections:

Keep looking in to the stomach

Keep pulling the the abs in, beginning the roll decrease again

from the abs

Keep the C curve within the spine

Roll down on the shoulder blades, maintain the top and

neck out of the mat!!!!

Clap the complete foot together

Keep the shoulders down

Notes:

When you have people with spinal troubles including scolioses you can not want to try this exercise. Instead you may do a roll up and down workout with the knees bend like a controlled crunch exercise.

Transition in to Push up series:

When you do your closing Seal, roll returned

Let the toes pass and in a single motion come to a status

feature

Without using fingers if you can, if no longer, use the palms

to rise up to a status function

Turn on the balls to ft to stand the top forestall of the

mat

Come to a Pilates stance

Push up series

Repetitions:

three instances

Goals:

Strengthen the abs

Strengthen fingers and shoulders

Set up:

Come to a Pilates stance

Lifting the fingers within the course of the ceiling

Shoulder down, ribs and abs pulled in

Set the workout in movement:

Roll down articulating the backbone

Hands flat at the floor ideally legs are still at once

(bend legs if wished)

Walk 3 steps with the fingers to a plank role

Push up 1, push up 2, push up 3 (breathe in even as

pushing down, breathe out while pushing up

Lift the butt to the ceiling (downwards dealing with dog)

And stroll the fingers over again in 3 steps

Articulating the backbone all over again as a good deal as a standing feature,

Pilates stance

Corrections:

Keep the feet in Pilates stance, hold heels collectively

Keep pulling the abs in

When rolling down articulate the spine

In plank feature preserve pushing the top lower once more in the route of

the ceiling

Squeeze the butt muscles in plank and push up

feature

Keep the elbows in the waist in push up

Long neck in plank, push up function and downwards

going through dog

Remind the breath

Notes:

If your university students are not strong sufficient allow them to located down the knees at the same time as doing the frenzy up or permit them to positioned down the knees and without a doubt hold the posture.

Finish in a sturdy Pilates stance.

These are all the Classical Pilates mat beginners sporting sports activities. Really examine the images in this ebook and the movement photos on the YouTube Channel

Classical Pilates. I hope to have cherished your Classical Pilates journey up to now.

eight. Terminology List

Pilates stance (ft grew to become out, 2 fists between feet)

Ballet first position (Legs turn out as a long manner as they can while maintaining instantly legs and straight decrease lower again, knees trouble in the same route because of the truth the feet)

Chapter 9: Background And Origins Of Pilates

It is essential to have a robust knowledge of the severa statistics and origins of the Pilates physical sports as a manner to have a whole appreciation for their electricity and effectiveness. Pilates, which become advanced with the aid of Joseph Pilates within the early twentieth century, isn't only a manner of working out; as a substitute, it's far a holistic system that represents the merger of Eastern and Western mind, drawing idea from severa disciplines which encompass yoga, martial arts, and gymnastics. Pilates have become now not only a exercise approach at the same time as it have grow to be advanced; as an opportunity, it come to be a machine that embodied the fusion of Eastern and Western philosophies.

Joseph Pilates, who have become born in Germany in 1883, turn out to be a innovative and innovative truth seeker who modified into many years earlier of his time. As a infant, he suffered from a number of bodily issues, which includes bronchial allergic reactions, rickets, and others. As a stop quit end result, he made it his assignment to enhance his personal health and health. In the path of his travels, he participated in a big form of sports activities sports activities and activities, at the side of bodybuilding, wrestling, and diving, all of which had an impact at the formation of his exercise normal.

Pilates changed into incarcerated as a prisoner of struggle at some stage in World War I, and it come to be there that he started out honing his strategies thru teaching different prisoners a manner to workout on the equal time as using bed springs as a form of resistance. These early experiments with gadget laid the inspiration for the improvement of the distinct Pilates gadget that is commonly used these days. These quantities of equipment encompass the Reformer, Cadillac, and Wunda Chair, among others.

Joseph Pilates made his home in New York City after arriving within the United States as a refugee in some unspecified time in the future of World War II. In the number one studio they ever opened, which became really referred to as "Pilates Studio," Joseph Pilates and his spouse Clara added a in advance-wondering method of bodily interest and rehabilitation that they called Pilates. The studio right now garnered a recognition for excellence among dancers, athletes, and specific people who've been inquisitive about improving their degree of physical fitness and regular health.

Joseph Pilates refers to his method as "Contrology," with the intention of highlighting the significance of retaining aware manipulate and precision for the period of every and every motion. He modified into of the opinion that humans also can gain a country that is harmonious and optimally wholesome in the occasion that they integrate their minds with their our bodies and spirits. His ideas, which encompass hobby, centering, breath, precision, manage, and flowing motion, consist of the clean basis of Pilates sports activities activities and are crucial to their effectiveness. He named those prinAthletes, celebrities, and normal people all use it to decorate their everyday power, flexibility, posture, and bodily normal performance. It has grow to be a stylish in the challenge of health.Ciples "The Seven Principles of Pilates."

Pilates is a shape of exercise that can be useful to human beings of many a long term and ranges of bodily fitness, and as a surrender stop result, it has amassed an significant quantity of recognition over the direction of its information. It has emerge as a tremendous inside the location of fitness and is utilized by athletes, celebrities, and normal human beings alike to enhance famous strength, flexibility, posture, and physical usual typical overall performance.

We are going to delve further into the necessities and techniques that strain the

Pilates approach as we maintain via this e-book. We will check the development and development of the Pilates technique inside the route of information, starting with the fundamentals of respiration and alignment and progressing to the best specifics of each workout. You will increase a profound appreciation for the reworking impact that Pilates might also ought to your frame, mind, and spirit in case you study its roots and its underlying philosophy. This will let you really take gain of the benefits that Pilates can offer you.

Let's get commenced out on this informative voyage through the deep records and roots of Pilates, and discover how its time-tested thoughts also can moreover alter your lifestyles and bring about a greater experience of equilibrium, energy, and popular properly-being.

The Philosophy of Pilates

The profound philosophy that underpins the Pilates approach can be stated to go past nicely past the vicinity of traditional bodily interest. Joseph Pilates emerge as of the opinion that real fitness and fitness require now not fine a robust and nimble frame but additionally an unruffled and intent thoughts so you may be finished. His philosophy, which is grounded in mind together with the thoughts-body connection and holistic dwelling, is at the coronary heart of the reworking capability of the Pilates approach.

Integration of the Mind and Body: Pilates places a strong emphasis on bringing collectively the practitioner's mind and body in each and each movement. It fosters a strong connection among intellectual attention and bodily hobby, encouraging mindfulness and focus even as it's far going approximately its art work. Pilates practitioners benefit heightened body interest and manage due to establishing this thoughts-frame connection, which lets in them to carry out movements that are every more efficient and particular.

Core Strength and Stability: The core is the center of manage and energy inside the body. In Pilates, the term "Powerhouse" is frequently used to refer to the core. Joseph Pilates held the perception that a sturdy center end up crucial for accomplishing one's complete ability in terms of every physical overall performance and traditional fitness. Pilates moves are designed to purpose and beautify the deep belly muscle mass, back muscles, and pelvic floor, which eventually ends up in the introduction of a sturdy and balanced basis that facilitates the frame in the course of all sports.

The significance of correct respiration as a foundational factor of Pilates can't be overstated. Joseph Pilates placed a strong emphasis on the use of diaphragmatic respiration and integrating it with movement an extraordinary way to decorate oxygenation, waft, and ordinary energy go along with the waft. The practice of aware respiratory now not best gives the frame with the strength it dreams but moreover encourages relaxation, interest, and a discount in stress.

Accuracy and Mastery: The Pilates technique emphasizes the top notch of motion over the quantity of motion achieved. Each exercising is done with a deft touch, a revel in of manage, and beauty. Joseph Pilates concept that human beings may additionally furthermore release their body's whole potential and avoid unneeded pressure or damage via appearing moves with mindfulness and hobby to element. Joseph Pilates advanced his technique to teach people the way to try this.

Flexibility and Postural Alignment: The reason of Pilates is to increase sort of movement, in addition to flexibility and postural alignment. Pilates sports activities paintings to repair balance and harmony inside the body with the aid of using manner of lengthening and stretching muscle businesses, ligaments, and fascia. This method permits to elongate and stretch the muscle tissues. The emphasis located on accurate alignment enables to guarantee that motions are done with ideal biomechanics, which in turn allows to reduce the risk of imbalances at the equal time as additionally fostering great posture and body mechanics.

Pilates is a holistic technique to physical health and widespread fitness and well-being. It works the body as an entire. It places an emphasis now not absolutely on someone's physical energy and flexibility however additionally on highbrow clarity, the cut rate of pressure, and emotional equilibrium. Pilates practitioners regularly record feelings of revitalization, better self-focus, and an simple experience of well-being because of the workout's emphasis on nourishing the body-mind connection.

The guiding principle of Joseph Pilates extends a long way past the sector of bodily interest and into all aspects of life. We can create mindfulness, resilience, and an unshakeable willpower to our personal properly-being if we combine the necessities of Pilates into our every day physical games and sports.

In the following chapters, we shall inspect, in more detail, the suitable mind and procedures that include the Pilates technique. You will drift on a innovative adventure this is going an extended way beyond physical fitness when you maintain near and encompass the philosophy underlying Pilates. This will assist you to increase harmony, stability, and power in all part of your existence.

PRINCIPLES OF PILATES

The six necessities of Pilates—Breath, Concentration, Control, Precision, Center, and Flow—were now not within the starting evolved via way of Joseph Pilates but rather by way of using his students. In order to simplify his technique and make it extra approachable for university university students of the future, they reduced his theories into six vital mind.

Because of the way in which the ones six standards have been developed, there can be excellent dialogue inside the Pilates network over the titles of the mind and the form of them.

Although they now and again undergo specific names, the bulk of Pilates instructors concur that there are six center mind or critical necessities in Pilates.

Pilates as it is practiced now, along aspect the six requirements:

Since Joseph first commenced out coaching in the 1920s, there has been a substantial boom in our expertise of human anatomy further to the workings of the transferring body.

In that time period, there has also been a shift in how Pilates is used.

Pilates is increasingly generally used as a primary trouble inside the rehabilitation of sufferers who have sustained maximum critical injuries. In addition, Pilates is often used to help clients decorate their not unusual physical situation. This often necessitates making huge modifications to the carrying sports and moving a protracted manner from the equal antique repertory.

Having stated all of this, and irrespective of all the breakthroughs that have been made in medical studies, even modern-day-day Pilates stays basically devoted to those six key pillars.

As if we desired any extra proof, proper here it's far: Joseph turn out to be a man who lived centuries in advance than his time.

In this segment, we delve deeper into the ones six guiding mind. At Complete Pilates, we compare them in moderate of the medical literature and speak the effects that their findings have for our exercise.

The 6 Core Principles of Pilates:

1. BREATH

First and essential, Pilates is all about the breath.

When most people reflect onconsideration on Pilates, the "hundreds" workout—characterized by using a strong inhale and exhale—is the primary aspect that involves thoughts.

Because of this, the truth that "breath" grow to be one of the maximum critical elements of Pilates for Joseph want to no longer come as a surprise.

According to a quotation attributed to him, he allegedly said, "Breathing is the primary act of life and the ultimate..Most importantly, discover ways to breathe efficaciously."

At Complete Pilates, we place the equal emphasis on right breathing as Joseph Pilates did. Joseph changed right into a pioneer in the vicinity. But manner to the finofade in scientific research, we now understand the correct purpose why it is so critical to have healthful breathing.

Incorrect breathing styles will have an impact on each place of the body. From inflicting neurological sensitivity to exacerbating posture troubles to having an effect at the fitness of our pelvic ground, the outcomes are big. Therefore, making enhancements to them has the capacity to significantly enhance our health.

The manner that we breathe also can have an effect on our functionality for movement.

If you keep your breath while looking for to twist your body, you could no longer get very an extended manner. However, if you breathe in deeply and without a doubt, your diaphragm can be capable to help you in doing this motion more with out issues.

When appearing belly sports activities sports, taking a forceful exhale additionally may be useful in activating the ones important deep middle muscle mass, which might be difficult to gain.

Recent research on mindfulness and meditation demonstrates that the intellectual benefits of growing healthful respiration practices in reality can not be overstated.

It has been verified that the thoughts gets signs to relax even as a person takes a slow, deep breath. This shows that developing healthy respiratory styles thru Pilates can make contributions to a discount in strain.

Both our bodily and emotional nicely-being are intertwined and can't be separated.

It need to therefore come as no marvel that one of the most essential elements of supporting humans in wearing out their dreams is instructing them in right respiratory techniques. Whether it's miles the restoration from an harm or simply an commonplace improvement in bodily fitness,

Principles of Pilates: Breathing: A lean woman sitting bypass-legged on a mat together with her wrists on her knees, fingers going via upward, and the thumb and arms of each hand touching

The Fundamentals of Pilates: Focus on Breathing

2. CONCENTRATION

Anyone who has ever participated in Pilates might be conscious that this fashion of workout requires one's full hobby always. Try to maintain your pelvis completely nevertheless and your shoulders relaxed as you move your legs round within the air. You are starting to understand.

However, "interest" meant more than genuinely the attention that was required to successfully do every exercise for Joseph.

In truth, he grow to be of the opinion that it became vital for his university college students to area a full-size quantity of interest at the movements that their our our bodies had been carrying out so as for them to enjoy the highbrow and bodily blessings that Pilates has to provide.

Joseph seemed to be one step in advance of clearly everyone else whilst it came to this unique element of Complete Pilates.

We now understand, because of a present day clinical have a have a study that has been done on mindfulness and meditation2, that some styles of "aware motion" can help lessen stress, decrease blood strain, and beautify our potential to cope with and control ache.

When you are appearing the Pilates sporting sports, it is to your first-class hobby to recognition on your body in preference to, for instance, the food you ate for breakfast. This has a number of extra blessings.

You can learn how to revel in in which you're transferring from and what muscle corporations are operating in case you direct your interest inward and awareness on your very personal sensations. Because of this, your body recognition will increase, and this may help you become more powerful inside the actions you do on a ordinary foundation, whether you are sitting at a desk all day or you're education for a half of marathon.

At Complete Pilates, we see this heightened body recognition as a extremely good technique for people to discover ways to rest their muscle businesses in addition to spark off them. This is one of the many blessings that people gain from schooling Pilates.

It is common to connect Pilates with "sucking in" the stomach muscle organizations or "lifting" the pelvic ground; although, we experience that it's far in addition as crucial to learn how to launch, to soften, and to let pass so one can sell desired bodily health.

three.CENTERING

There is a connection between the concept of the "powerhouse" in Pilates and the concept of the center.

In Joseph's mind, this location of the body became fashioned like a discipline that extended from the shoulders all of the way right all of the manner all the way down to the vicinity clearly below the hip joints at the the front of the body and the lowest of your backside on the decrease again. The moves that make up the Pilates repertoire are speculated to be finished the use of this "discipline" because the start line.

In order to prompt this location, your teachers may also additionally cue you to "scoop in" or "hole" your abdominals.

Although the ones cues are given with the superb of intentions (to protect your decrease once more, tone your abdominals, and set off your middle), they're able to sincerely have a unfavourable impact on the frame.

At Complete Pilates:

We now have a higher understanding of why those cues won't constantly be very useful because of the enhancements which have been made in scientific research, like this check approximately how seeking out to raise your pelvic floor can bring about you pushing it down.

Chapter 10: Benefits Of Pilates

The call Pilates is now acquainted to nearly absolutely everyone because of the lengthy, lean, and sculpted look that can be completed via the exercise of Pilates.

There is a lot greater to it than the overly simplistic advertising that encourages a "extended and lean" form, and there may be also more to it than the notion that it is commonly for women.

No rely their gender, age, race, duration, potential, or cutting-edge degree of fitness, in reality everybody can have interplay in Pilates as a form of exercise.

There are over 600 specific exercises and variations which may be part of the Pilates repertoire. These bodily games may be completed on a mat or at the ground. No rely their gender, age, race, duration, capability, or modern-day diploma of fitness, each person can engage in Pilates as a form of workout. Specialized system.

There is a few difficulty suitable for every person, regardless of whether or not or not they lead a sedentary lifestyle, compete in weekend tournaments, are pregnant, are going via rehabilitation, be bothered through anxiety, or are expert athletes.

Studies have proven that Pilates has a favorable effect on despair further to ache, most significantly a lower in lower back pain. This contributes to an everyday development in incredible of existence.

Other advantages encompass the following:

1. It improves center energy

The "center" of the body, also referred to as the "powerhouse," from which all movement originates, is the number one attention of the Pilates exercise technique. The term "center" refers back to the group of muscle businesses that surround the trunk and serve to help and stabilize the frame while they're each strong and flexible.

Strength and function inside the middle may be improved with Pilates . Core power is an essential detail in lowering the danger of experiencing again and hip pain, similarly to decreasing the possibility of experiencing pelvic floor problems. This area is likewise the supply of explosive movement, earning it the moniker "the powerhouse."

2. It makes one's posture look better

When your mother and father endorsed you to prevent slouching and sit up, they have been at the right track with their advice.

A better posture should make the difference among having susceptible muscle mass, muscular imbalances, headaches, shoulder or lower back pain, and being able to take a seat or stand erect without problem.

Pilates locations an emphasis on proper alignment within the course of the whole frame, an most nice variety of motion on the joints, and a balanced contraction of all opposing muscle tissue. It does this with the useful aid of making you greater aware of your alignment and thru strengthening the postural muscular tissues which may be regularly not noted. The stop result is an development on your posture.

3. It alleviates the pain in the returned.

A actual indication of power is the potential of the deeper stomach muscles and the pelvic floor muscular tissues to every settlement and loosen up while acting Pilates. These muscle corporations perform the function of a brace by means of the use of lifting and assisting the organs, similarly to protective and stabilizing the once more.

four. It protects users from getting damage.

Pilates works to create equilibrium within the body's muscular tissues, ensuring that they will be neither slack and floppy nor traumatic and inflexible. It is possible for the body to emerge as more vulnerable to damage if the muscles are either too free and willing or too stiff and rigid.

The primary purpose of Pilates is to help you increase your dynamic electricity, which will increase your functionality to assist and stabilize your joints whilst you are in motion. Research has tested that Pilates is an powerful approach for lowering the hazard of becoming injured at the same time as taking part in athletics.-

five. It outcomes in an growth in electricity

Pilates can boom one's cardiorespiratory functionality as it places an emphasis on respiratory. This will boom the float of feel-tremendous hormones in addition to oxygen and circulation inside the blood.

Pilates accomplishes all of these goals similarly to leaving you feeling plenty much much less weary than different styles of exercising because of its low impact nature. Instead, it gives you with an boom on your energy stages.

6. It improves one's interest in their own our our bodies

Proprioception, moreover called body recognition, can be improved through the thoughts-body exercise of Pilates.

Your recognition of ache or satisfaction, your emotions, and the sector round you're all better while you direct your interest inward and are capable of cope with the sensations which are taking area inside your body.

Increased proprioception gives the frame a extra functionality to answer to stimuli, which in turn makes it greater proof against accidents and unintentional falls. If you've got a higher hobby of your body, you may be more in music with the signs that your frame sends out when it's miles hungry , which can also even assist you avoid overeating.

7. It effects in a discount of strain

The inward interest that Pilates requires, collectively with using breath, can help to reduce the interest of the anxious device, that is a continuation of one of the benefits of prolonged bodily focus. This, in turn, can pull you out of the "fight or flight" phase, drop cortisol, and reduce stress over the route of time.

8. It eases the pain related to menstruation

If you have ever suffered from the contamination known as dysmenorrhea, which reasons painful menstrual cycles, then you definitely absolutely have firsthand understanding of methods incapacitating the scenario can be. There is some evidence that Pilates may be capable of help ease the soreness associated with menstruation.

9. It enhances the body's flexibility and adaptableness.

First matters first, allow's speak about the difference amongst mobility and flexibility.

The degree to which a muscle can also additionally stretch without actively doing so is called its flexibility. Mobility refers back to the volume to which a joint is capable of skip. Not only flexibility but also strength is crucial for unique mobility.

While flexibility in and of itself isn't always continually useful, mobility is some thing that you need to aspire to gain. To get maximum mobility, you have to strike a healthy stability among your strength and versatility education.

A Pilates exercise is constantly moving, with fluid transitions among gradual, controlled motions and ones which might be greater specific. The majority of the actions in Pilates are a aggregate of strengthening and stretching, which allows growth strength, flexibility, and mobility.

Stretching is normally completed after a strengthening exercise.

10. It makes one more balanced.

Balance is essential for all of us, no matter age, due to the fact it's far required for sports that require coordination on a ordinary foundation, which encompass on foot, in addition to for any of lifestyles's nonlinear actions, including achieving up and twisting.

Pilates now not first-rate strengthens the middle, however it furthermore makes a speciality of alignment and moves that artwork the complete body.

Both of these elements make a contribution to an development in stability and gait.

eleven. It strengthens your resistance to infection.

There is evidence that Pilates can improve the functioning of the immune system, specifically in individuals who are older.

However, regardless of the truth that almost all of have a have a observe has been done on people in their later years, those findings display that people of any age ought to enjoy the immune device enhancement that Pilates offers, in most instances due to better flow into.

The feature of the immune system is also prolonged with the development in move. Pilates improves the motion of blood and lymph, every of which may be essential for a healthful immune device. A healthful immune machine is a characteristic of a successfully functioning blood and lymph device.

12. It has a splendid impact on cognitive functioning.

Pilates education has been verified to result in higher cognitive functioning in research research.

A range of markers, consisting of new neuron formation, blood flow to the thoughts, extra quality neurotransmitters, and the life of neurons critical for getting to know, reminiscence, and government questioning, have been evaluated.

thirteen. It has the capacity to decorate one's motivation.

Pilates turn out to be determined to be beneficial in one test for reinforcing university college students' motivation, similarly to its effectiveness for enhancing college students' cognition.

In every different have a look at, the researchers seemed into the sorts of motivation that pressure human beings to exercising Pilates and came to the belief that these humans are extra motivated via their non-public intrinsic motivation than by using the use of the outdoor validation they gather from others.

14. It makes your sexual lifestyles better.

Pilates has many advantages, one in every of this is that it is able to make time spent inside the sack extra interesting.. To start, it improves your stamina, energy, mobility, and flexibility, all of which allow you to have more amusing inside the mattress room via technique of making it much less tough at the manner to get into positions and stay there for longer.

Chapter 11: Pilates Method

Joseph Pilates is credited with developing a way of workout and bodily conditioning that is generally known as "Pilates in the early 20th century. This method is known as the Pilates Method. It is an all-encompassing technique of physical exercising that places an emphasis on improving flexibility, growing more body interest and manipulate, and working to bolster the center muscle groups.

Joseph Pilates termed his method "Contrology" while he first superior it as it locations a strong emphasis on the use of intellectual recognition to control physical motion. The Pilates Method is based on a hard and fast of crucial requirements that serve to direct the exercising and assure the technique's fulfillment. As have become stated in advance than, the subsequent thoughts fall under this elegance: centering, interest, manipulate, precision, breath, and waft.

The Pilates Method consists of a huge type of wearing sports that can be finished on a mat or with expert machine which consist of the reformer, Cadillac, and Pilates chair. These wearing sports are performed on the mat. The deep muscle mass of the belly, again, hips, and buttocks, which can be collectively known as the "powerhouse" or the middle, are the focus of the sporting events. They are designed to reason the ones muscle tissues.

The sporting sports in Pilates location an emphasis on correct alignment, retaining stability, and moving in a controlled way. They frequently want activation of the belly muscle mass, coordination of the breath, and the protection of actions that are each fluid and accurate. The sports activities of Pilates may be altered to cater to a high-quality fashion of potential gadgets and stages of physical fitness, making the workout on hand to human beings of numerous a long time and tiers of mobility.

The Pilates Method have end up superior with the intention of improving someone's revel in of well-being in addition to their strength, flexibility, balance, and posture. Pilates, at the equal time as practiced on a ordinary basis, has the potential to result in a more potent and extra toned body, in addition to better body interest, superior coordination, and a decrease chance of accidents.

Pilates is well-known for its emphasis on mindfulness and the thoughts-body connection, similarly to the useful effects it has on someone's physique. It promotes relaxation, stress cut price, and highbrow readability with the resource of encouraging practitioners to be totally present in the motions themselves, encouraging full presence.

Those from all walks of life, together with athletes, dancers, those in want of rehabilitation, and people attempting to find a extra holistic method to fitness, are some of the humans who've taken up the Pilates

Method as a shape of exercise as it has received popularity the world over. It is often taught in a hard and fast placing or via one-on-one sessions with a knowledgeable Pilates teacher who directs and corrects the method used at some diploma inside the bodily sports activities.

The Pilates Method as an entire is an all-encompassing form of exercise that consists of manage, strength, flexibility, and mindfulness training to enhance one's bodily fitness similarly to their mental and emotional u . S ..

MAT PILATE

Mat Pilates is a shape of exercising that specializes in your center (trunk) muscle groups on the same time as simultaneously exercising your legs and arms. It is a form of exercising this is every strengthening and increasing. Joseph Pilates invented the sports activities that would later become called mat Pilates on the manner to beef up his very non-public frame at the same time as he modified proper into a more youthful guy. Pilates Mat art work is the muse of Pilates and became superior extended in advance than any of the Pilates gadget or "machines" that are used inside the scenario nowadays. It consists of over 500 bodily activities that may be completed anywhere. Mat Pilates may be tailor-made to house individuals of any age, frame type, or fitness level; it is also possible to perform changed mat physical activities even as seated in a chair.

The Advantages of Practicing Pilates on a Mat

Enhanced posture, extra suitable coordination and balance, greater lung capability, stepped forward awareness and cognizance, accelerated frame consciousness, stress manage, and damage avoidance are a number of the advantages that may be attained through the workout of Pilates, that could be a exercise that engages the mind, the body, and the spirit. Mat paintings is an extraordinary alternative for Pilates practitioners of all tiers because of the reality not satisfactory may additionally moreover the sporting activities upward thrust in trouble, but each workout can also be tweaked to decrease or beautify the level of assignment. Because of these factors, mat paintings is an extraordinary possibility. Mat Pilates allows to construct a sturdy, well-balanced body and enhances flexibility while practiced often. As your degree of exercising will boom, you turns into extra aware about enhancements for your breathing, recognition, and frame consciousness. Because you in fact want your personal body, a mat, and a few ground space to get commenced out out with mat Pilates, it's far a great form of exercise for novices.

A Few Pointers and Suggestions for Novices

Mat Those who are new to the Pilates exercising can bear in mind taking issue in a Pilates consultation. Professional Pilates approach teachers are in rate of both organization training and private instructions at Pilates studios and some other varieties of health centers. You moreover have the option of starting a exercising at domestic with the help of books, movies, or on line streaming applications which encompass Pilates Anytime. Take it sluggish, and do now not assume that you will be running the equal muscle corporations you have been on foot in conjunction with your preceding types of exercise honestly because of the reality you are doing the identical aspect. Try not to get frustrated in case you are not capable of perform every exercising to the exceptional of your functionality. There is a splendid cause why Pilates is known as a exercise: performing the sporting sports effectively takes attention and willpower. In order a fantastic manner to carry out the sporting sports inside the right way, you want to offer your self permission to gradual down and make the actions smaller. To get commenced, you have to pick out out to visit magnificence as a minimum instances consistent with week and have no hassle getting at the mat and trying some of the movements on the identical time as you are at home.

Avoiding Common Errors Made thru the usage of Beginners on the Mat

Do your excellent no longer to experience pissed off as you begin your Pilates workout; the exercising locations a easy emphasis on your frame and the way it actions. We regularly lose sight of the motive of the workout because of the fact we each float too fast or try and create huge movements. Reduce the dimensions of every person movement.

Keep in mind that while you are moving one part of your frame, you also are striving to stabilize every one of a kind issue. If it seems as despite the fact that all of your strive is leg labor, you need to lessen the amount of labor and address your respiration in addition to the activation of your stomach muscle mass. Don't forget about about to breathe; the try you're making along with your breath makes up a full-size piece of finding the right diploma of willpower. At first, cues which includes "sink your stomach button into your backbone" might not make a good buy feel to you.

On the opportunity hand, the cue refers to the feeling of letting your ribs lighten up closer to your hips whilst pulling your belly button toward your spine on an exhale to interact your belly muscular tissues. This is executed on the identical time as maintaining a impartial backbone feature. Despite the reality that your pelvis may not drift or tilt, you will enjoy a pulling up of your pelvic floor muscles, which is probably your decrease abdominals (expect under the hips). Pilates is not going to return again decrease lower back virtually to you right away, and this is perfectly outstanding! Give yourself permission to take satisfaction in the technique of coming across new matters about your frame and finding new methods to move. Have an high-quality time with it!

EQUIPMENT-BASED PILATES

Equipment-based totally Pilates is the decision given to the exercising technique superior via using Joseph Pilates and carried out on expert tool synthetic with the aid of the use of Joseph Pilates himself. These quantities of gadget provide extra resistance, guide, and assist, which lets in to maximise the blessings that can be received from the sporting sports activities.

Equipment-primarily based honestly Pilates makes use of an entire lot of exceptional forms of device, along with the following:

The reformer is one of the portions of Pilates device this is utilized the most regularly. It is constituted of a sliding carriage this is secured to a frame with the aid of pulleys, springs, and straps. When the practitioner does carrying sports activities, the springs offer numerous resistance to the practitioner, which serves to decorate and stretch muscle groups on the equal time as additionally difficult the practitioner's balance and manipulate.

The Cadillac, moreover known as the trapeze table, is a large framework that includes an multiplied platform, bars, straps, and comes.

It is occasionally cited by means of the use of way of its opportunity call, the Cadillac. It gives a numerous form of sporting sports that can be performed in hundreds of positions, along side seated, reputation, or mendacity down. As a quit give up result of the brought assist, resistance, and help that it offers, the Cadillac is nicely-relevant for use in rehabilitation settings further to greater superior Pilates bodily games.

A compact piece of system, the Pilates chair, furthermore referred to as the Wunda Chair or the Exo Chair, the chair includes a seat and foot pedal or pedals. Other names for the chair consist of the Exo Chair and the Wunda Chair. A large sort of sports activities activities that focus on stability, electricity, and stability may be completed inside the chair. These sports aim the entire body.

Pilates barrels are to be had in some of sizes and configurations, together with the backbone corrector, ladder barrel, and arc barrel, among others. Stretching, spinal mobility, and strengthening carrying sports are all supported thru manner of these pieces of kit, with a unique consciousness at the decrease back, shoulders, and hips.

Tower/Wall Unit: The tower or wall unit is a bit of kit that may be located on the wall and includes factors of the reformer, the Cadillac, and unique portions of Pilates system. It includes springs, bars, straps, and handles, which together make it viable to do a sizeable shape of exercises that concentrate on excellent groups of muscle tissues.

Pilates tool-based totally completely classes commonly have a licensed Pilates instructor number one them and take area in a studio or each one-of-a-kind region created mainly for the exercise of Pilates. The teacher gives individualized schooling, making any critical changes to the settings of the equipment and providing direct, arms-on path to assure correct posture, form, and alignment.

Equipment-based definitely absolutely Increased resistance, assist for perfect alignment, and additional range inside the carrying sports are the numerous specific benefits that may be won from schooling Pilates. It allows contemporary challenges and customization to in shape the needs of people at specific health stages or human beings with precise desires or constraints. Specifically, it could meet the needs of people with unique objectives or policies.

Both the mat-based and device-based definitely versions of Pilates adhere to the same important tenets, which is probably together called the Pilates requirements. These standards embody centering, attention, manage, precision, breath, and go together with the glide. The choice amongst mat Pilates and Pilates the usage of gadget is one which need to be made relying on the person's alternatives, the supply of tool, and their precise health desires.

BASIC PILATES EXERCISES

The following is a listing of physical video games that are crucial to Pilates and can be accomplished on a mat or with very little machine:

Lie in your once more at the side of your knees bent and your ft planted firmly at the ground to begin The Hundred. Raise your head, neck, and shoulders off the mat, and attain your hands alongside the perimeters of your body at the identical time as doing so. While you inhale for 5 counts and exhale for 5 counts, flow into your hands up and down at your factors in a pumping motion. Continue in this manner for a whole of ten devices and one hundred reps.

Lie for your once more along side your knees bent and your shins parallel to the ground. This is the start position for the single-leg stretch. Bring the knee of one leg into your chest while extending the opportunity leg at a 45-degree attitude without delay out inside the front of you. To trade legs, definitely switch the location of your palms on every of your ankles on the same time. Repeat on each element for an entire of eight to ten times.

168

First, get proper into a bridge function via manner of lying for your once more along side your knees bent and your toes planted firmly on the floor. Put your arms down next on your factors. Raise your hips off the mat to form a line that is parallel to the floor out of your knees on your shoulders. Bring your hips all of the way back down to the mat on the equal time as maintaining manage. Continue on this way for 8–10 repetitions.

Begin in a push-up feature along with your arms placed squarely under your shoulders and your toes tucked beneath. This is the start characteristic for the plank. Engage your middle and glutes to hold a immediately line out of your head on your heels at the same time as you perform the workout. Maintain this stance for twenty to thirty seconds whilst bringing your hobby in your breath and your stability.

Lie on your stomach along side your fingers outstretched above your head. This is the start function for the swan dive. Raise your

169

pinnacle frame off the mat via the use of lifting your palms and chest on the equal time as concurrently extending your legs inside the back of you. Maintain a in advance stare while you increase, and stretch out your body as you accomplish that. Control the way you deliver your back down. Continue doing so for the following 6–eight repetitions.

Lifting the Legs While Lying on Your Side Lie to your thing together with your legs extended without delay out within the the front of you and stacked on pinnacle of each other. Put your head down to your lower arm, and rest the hand that is better in your frame at the ground within the the front of you for beneficial aid. Raise the pinnacle of your leg a few inches off the mat whilst retaining a immediately role. Bring it backpedal slowly at the same time as maintaining manage. Repeat on every component for an entire of 8 to 10 times.

Keep in thoughts that the physical video games shown right here are only a few samples of simple Pilates actions. It is essential that you keep your frame in the ideal function for the length of every exercising, be aware of your respiratory, and actively set off your middle muscle corporations so you can attain balance and control. It is pretty recommended that everyone who's new to Pilates exercising with a expert Pilates teacher. This individual can be able to educate you thru the sports activities and make certain which you are finishing them successfully.

HUNDRED

The Hundred is a traditional Pilates workout that specializes in enticing the center muscles and growing bypass and breath manipulate. Here's a way to carry out The Hundred:

1. Start through mendacity in your again on a mat collectively together with your knees bent and feet flat at the ground. Make exceptional your backbone is in a impartial feature, with a natural curve on your decrease again.

2. Bring your knees in the direction of your chest, lifting your ft off the floor. Your knees need to be located right away above your hips, forming a tabletop function along with your legs.

3. Inhale deeply, making equipped for the exercise. As you exhale, boost your head, neck, and shoulders off the mat, reaching your chin inside the path of your chest. Keep your gaze focused in your abdominals.

four. Extend your arms along your body, hands dealing with down. Lift your hands a few inches off the mat, preserving them immediately and conducting toward your feet.

Chapter 12: What Is Wall Pilates?

Wall Pilates is a shape of Pilates exercise this is finished with the help of a wall or distinct vertical floor. It is a low-effect shape of exercise that focuses on center and posture strengthening, flexibility, and stability. This method of workout is useful for those who've physical barriers, collectively with accidents or persistent ache, as well as for individuals who are new to Pilates.

Benefits of Wall Pilates for Seniors

1. Improved stability and coordination: Wall Pilates can assist seniors beautify their balance and coordination, which can assist reduce their risk of falling.

2. Strengthened muscle mass: Wall Pilates can assist beautify the middle muscle groups, as well as one-of-a-type muscle tissues inside the frame, that could assist lessen pain and assist seniors preserve their mobility.

three. Improved flexibility: Wall Pilates can help enhance flexibility, which could help improve variety of movement and reduce stiffness.

four. Improved posture: Wall Pilates can help seniors enhance their posture, that can help alleviate once more pain and decorate normal fitness.

5. Improved intellectual readability: Wall Pilates can help seniors beautify their intellectual readability and attention, that can help lessen pressure and enhance ordinary well-being.

6. Improved go with the flow: Wall Pilates can assist seniors enhance their pass, that could help lessen fatigue and decorate fashionable fitness.

7. Low effect workout: Wall Pilates is a low impact form of workout, which can help lessen the stress on joints and muscle corporations, and help seniors get the exercise they need with out putting too much stress on their body.

eight. Reduced threat of damage: Wall Pilates can help lessen the risk of damage and assist seniors stay safe at the identical time as exercising.

9. Fun and Social: Wall Pilates may be amusing and social, and might help seniors live engaged and lively.

10. Convenience: Wall Pilates can be performed at home or in a health club, making it a to be had form of workout for seniors.

Basic Wall Pilates Workout for Seniors

1. Standing Pilates Twist: Stand with ft hip width aside and fingers extended out to elements. Twist better body to the right, bringing left hand to right thigh. Hold for three deep breaths, then transfer aspects.

2. Chair Squat: Stand with ft hip width aside, decrease again in opposition to a wall. Lower into a squat function, preserving again towards the wall and knees over your feet. Hold for 3 deep breaths, then stand again up.

three. Wall Pushups: Place palms at the wall, shoulder width aside, and step feet lower returned so body is in a right away line. Bend elbows and decrease chest closer to the wall. Hold for three deep breaths, then thrust back up.

four. Wall Sit: Stand with feet hip width aside and again in the route of the wall. Slide down the wall until thighs are parallel to the ground. Hold for three deep breaths, then stand yet again up.

5. Wall Triceps Dips: Place hands at the wall, shoulder width aside, and step ft decrease again so body is in a immediately line. Bend elbows and reduce body within the course of the ground. Hold for 3 deep breaths, then ward off up.

6. Wall Plank: Place fingers at the wall, shoulder width apart, and step toes lower decrease returned so frame is in a right away line. Hold for 3 deep breaths, then decrease proper proper down to knees.

7. Wall Bridge: Lie flat at the floor with toes in competition to the wall. Push into the wall to raise hips off the ground, forming a bridge. Hold for 3 deep breaths, then lower down.

8. Wall Side Plank: Place proper elbow at the wall, shoulder width apart. Step ft returned so body is in a right now line. Hold for three deep breaths, then switch elements.

nine. Wall Hamstring Hold: Lie flat at the ground with ft in competition to the wall. Push into the wall to reinforce hips off the ground, forming a bridge. Hold for 3 deep breaths, then decrease down.

10. Wall Calf Stretch: Stand coping with the wall and location fingers at the wall, shoulder width apart. Step proper foot lower returned, bending left knee and pushing hips in advance. Hold for three deep breaths, then switch components.

Chapter 13: Wall Pilates Workout For Senior Women

1. Seated Spine Twist (2 devices of 10 reps): Sit on the brink of a chair and interlock your hands in the returned of your head. Twist your frame to the proper, then to the left.

2. Kneeling Hip Flexor Stretch (2 gadgets of 10 reps): Kneel on one knee with the alternative leg extended out in the the front of you. Lean beforehand and press your hips forward until you experience a stretch within the the front of your hip.

three. Standing Glute Stretch (2 units of 10 reps): Stand collectively together with your ft hip width apart and slowly bend one leg back, maintaining your knee bent at 90 stages. Lean in advance until you experience a stretch on your glutes.

4. Seated Shoulder Shrugs (2 units of 10 reps): Sit getting ready to a chair and lift your shoulders up in the course of your ears. Hold for some seconds after which lower them go into reverse.

5. Chest Stretches (2 gadgets of 10 reps): Stand collectively with your hands outstretched inside the front of you and your hands going via up. Gently decrease your arms within the lower back of your again and keep for some seconds.

6. Wall Push-Ups (2 devices of 10 reps): Stand managing a wall and place your hands at the wall barely wider than shoulder-width aside. Bend your elbows and reduce your body within the path of the wall. Push yourself lower returned as plenty because the beginning position.

7. Seated Leg Raises (2 devices of 10 reps): Sit in a chair along side your legs prolonged inside the the front of you. Lift one leg up and maintain for some seconds. Slowly decrease it backtrack. Repeat with the opportunity leg.

8. Wall Squats (2 devices of 10 reps): Stand at the facet of your decrease decrease again towards a wall and your ft hip-width apart. Slowly bend your knees and reduce yourself towards the wall. Hold for some seconds after

which push your self decrease again as plenty due to the fact the starting role.

9. Standing Hamstring Stretch (2 gadgets of 10 reps): Stand with one foot beforehand and the opportunity foot in the back of you. Keeping your lower again right away, bend your the the front knee and slowly lean your top frame ahead until you enjoy a stretch within the lower back of your leg. Switch legs and repeat.

10. Seated Core Crunch (2 gadgets of 10 reps): Sit in a chair at the side of your ft flat on the ground and your hands at the back of your head. Gently increase your shoulders off the chair and crunch your abs inside the course of your backbone. Hold for some seconds after which decrease your body go into reverse.

Chapter 14: Exercises To Beautify Balance And Flexibility

1. Single Leg Balance: Stand on one foot and increase the possibility leg out within the front of you. Hold this role for 30 seconds and transfer legs.

2. Butterfly Stretch: Sit on the floor and produce the soles of your feet collectively. Pull your toes in as near your body as you may and hold for 30 seconds.

3. Standing Side Stretch: Stand up instantly collectively along with your feet barely wider than shoulder-width apart. Reach your palms up over your head and attain one arm up and the opportunity down. Hold for 30 seconds and switch factors.

four. Bridge Pose: Lie in your decrease again together in conjunction with your knees bent and ft flat at the floor. Lift your hips off the floor and hold for 30 seconds.

five. Plank: Get right proper right into a pushup characteristic together together with your palms without delay and your fingers right now underneath your shoulders. Hold for 30 seconds.

6. Hamstring Stretch: Lie on your decrease back with one leg extended immediately in the air. Wrap a towel or band throughout the ball of your foot and lightly pull the leg towards your head. Hold for 30 seconds and transfer legs.

7. Lunge: Step one leg in advance and bend both of your knees to a 90-diploma mind-set. Hold for 30 seconds and switch legs

8. Calf Stretch: Stand going through a wall and region your palms against it for aid. Place one foot in the front of the other and press your once more heel into the floor. Hold for 30 seconds and switch legs.

Targeted Strengthening Exercises

1. Glute Bridge: Lie on your again collectively collectively with your knees bent and your toes flat on the ground. Lift your hips off the floor and squeeze your glutes at the pinnacle

of the motion. Lower your hips backtrack to the floor.

2. Quadruped Hip Extension: Start in your hands and knees. Keep your middle engaged and your again flat. Lift one leg up off the floor and expand it immediately behind you. Return to the beginning characteristic.

3. Glute Kickback: Stand up and location your hands on a wall or counter for help. Bend one knee and raise your heel as immoderate as you can at the same time as keeping your ft pointed. Return to the beginning feature.

four. Clamshell: Lie on your problem collectively with your legs bent and your toes stacked. Lift your top knee up as excessive as you could even as maintaining your feet collectively. Lower your knee backpedal to the beginning function.

5. Calf Raises: Stand up together with your feet hip width apart. Lift your heels up off the ground as immoderate as you could. Lower your heels backtrack to the starting function.

Wall Pilates for Core and Posture Strengthening

1. Warm up: Start with the useful resource of lying on your returned, collectively together with your fingers outstretched, and your legs prolonged. Lift your legs up inside the air, after which lower them back off. Repeat this 10 times.

2. Scissors: Start via using lying to your lower lower back together with your legs at once. Lift one leg up after which the other, transferring them from side to side in a scissor like movement. Repeat this 10 instances.

3. Leg Lifts: Start through mendacity to your once more together with your legs without delay. Lift each legs up collectively as immoderate as you could, and then lower them backpedal. Repeat this 10 instances.